THE SOES BANDITS' GUIDE

DAY TRADING IN THE 21st CENTURY

**BY
HARVEY I. HOUTKIN
THE "ORIGINAL" SOES BANDIT**

COPYRIGHT 1995 - HARVEY I. HOUTKIN

ISBN 0-9647872-0-2

MAY NOT BE REPRODUCED IN WHOLE OR IN PART WITHOUT THE AUTHOR'S EXPRESS WRITTEN CONSENT

TABLE OF CONTENTS

ABOUT THE AUTHOR ii

AUTHOR'S ACKNOWLEDGEMENTS iii

DISCLAIMER iv

AUTHOR'S PREFACE v

CHAPTER ONE: INTRODUCTION 1

CHAPTER TWO: WHAT IS SOES TRADING? 8

CHAPTER THREE: ADVANTAGES OF SOES TRADING
                  OVER OTHER DAY TRADING 19

CHAPTER FOUR: IS SOES TRADING FOR YOU? 26

CHAPTER FIVE: HOW HAVE OTHER SOES TRADERS
                  FARED TO DATE? 31

CHAPTER SIX: WHAT DO I NEED TO
                  GET STARTED? 33

CHAPTER SEVEN: CHOOSING YOUR SOES FIRM 41

CHAPTER EIGHT: SOES TRADING TECHNIQUES 44

CHAPTER NINE: SPOTTING MARKET TRENDS 52

CHAPTER TEN: WIGGLES, JIGGLES & HEADFAKES 55

CHAPTER ELEVEN: EVALUATING THE MARKET MAKERS 62

CHAPTER TWELVE: WHICH ARE THE SOES STOCKS? 72

CHAPTER THIRTEEN: CONCLUSION 79

ABOUT THE AUTHOR

HARVEY I. HOUTKIN is the president of Domestic Securities, Inc. and the CEO of All-Tech Investment Group, Inc. Both firms have been in the forefront of the fight to have automated electronic execution systems and unrestricted competitive markets proliferate in the U.S. financial markets. Mr. Houtkin received his MBA in 1973 from the Bernard M. Baruch College of the City University of New York. His masters' degree thesis was titled "The Impact of Nasdaq on the OTC Securities Market." Until 1988, Mr. Houtkin was active in risk arbitrage, providing risk arbitrage services for such firms as Eastman Dillon, American Securities, Oppenheimer & Co., Icahn & Co., Arbitrage Securities Company and Domestic Arbitrage Group. During these years he was a member of the New York Stock Exchange, the American Stock Exchange and various commodity and regional exchanges. In 1988, he began utilizing the SOES system to enhance his success at All-Tech Investment Group, Inc. in his day trading endeavors. He is currently president of Domestic Securities, Inc., a firm that prides itself in cutting spreads to foster competition, and CEO of All-Tech Investment Group, Inc., a firm that is actively expanding the opportunities for SOES trading to the general public.

AUTHOR'S ACKNOWLEDGEMENTS

The author acknowledges his indebtedness to the individuals who contributed their input, suggestions and commentary to this project, but wishes to point out the invaluable assistance which was consistently provided with cheer and grace by Linda Lerner and Mark D. Shefts.

The author dedicates this book to his wife, Sherry D. Houtkin and his sister, Wanda D. Shefts.

Harvey I. Houtkin

Montvale, New Jersey
March 13, 1995

DISCLAIMER

THE OPINIONS EXPRESSED IN THIS GUIDE ARE THOSE OF THE AUTHOR. THERE CAN BE NO GUARANTEE OF SUCCESS. SOES TRADING IS NOT FOR EVERYONE. IT REQUIRES DRIVE, STAMINA, DISCIPLINE, AND THE ABILITY TO ALLOCATE FINANCIAL RESOURCES NOT NEEDED FOR OTHER PURPOSES, MONEY WHICH YOU CAN AFFORD TO LOSE. BECAUSE SOES TRADING USES MARGIN, IT IS POSSIBLE THAT LOSSES MAY EXCEED THE AMOUNT INVESTED.

AUTHOR'S PREFACE

Why should I bother to write a "how to guide" on a business career opportunity when my feeling has always been, if what an author has to say is so brilliant, why doesn't he just do it, become rich and to hell with everyone else. Exactly! So why this book? First of all, I was the "original" SOES bandit as detailed in an October 1988's Barrons article, "TERRORS OF THE TUBE." I have continued to SOES trade since 1988 along with my family and friends. My successes in this endeavor have been significant. So why invite competition into this wonderful field of opportunity? Simple - by myself and with only a few other participants the securities industry would have surely eliminated this niche. From 1988 to the present, the NASD has done everything in its power to stop me and put an end to SOES trading. Its tactics, which I believe are immoral, unbusinesslike, anti-competitive and probably illegal, are just now being investigated by the U.S. Department of Justice and the Securities and Exchange Commission.

My only hope for maintaining a safe environment for SOES trading is to increase the ranks of the SOES trading community. There is strength in numbers. Don't think I'm doing this just to be a nice guy or make a lot of money writing a book. My primary objective is to teach this technique to enough candidates to assure its perpetuity. If thousands of individuals choose to participate in the market by trading in this remarkable way, it will be much more difficult for a few corrupt regulators to stifle their attempts. So, do me and yourself a favor - understand what it is I am telling you, get started on an exciting, unbelievably rewarding career, and become a member of the SOES trading community.

The language in this book is like that in trading - simple and to the point. I have not filled this book with fluff, and I try to get to the point simply and directly. SOES trading is not complex and requires understanding a few simple concepts - read, understand, follow and prosper.

CHAPTER ONE

INTRODUCTION

You've read about me and my SOES trading techniques in Time Magazine, Forbes, Business Week, The New York Times, London Financial Times, The Los Angeles Times, The Wall Street Journal and virtually every other legitimate publication covering Wall Street or business news. You've seen me interviewed on television on shows such as Wall Street Journal Report, and on CNBC and even the BBC (British Broadcasting Corp.). Why all the interest? Well, some people claim I have found the key to the vault - Day Trading. Not just any day trading but day trading in Nasdaq stocks utilizing SOES (the NASD's computerized Small Order Execution System) and SelectNet (the NASD's computerized bid and offer system). Hello - I'm the one and only original "SOES BANDIT".

It may seem highly unusual for someone to wear the badge "Bandit" with pride, but in the crazy world of Wall Street strange things happen. "Bandit", "Shark", "Electronic Highwayman", "Scumbag", "Bastard" and "Roach" are just a few of the labels bestowed on me by my market making peers on Wall Street. The venom directed at me and my firms by the Nasdaq market making community and the NASD (National Association of Securities Dealers, Inc.) itself is probably unprecedented in the history of the U.S. financial markets.

Why have these terms been used in reference to my trading activities? It is quite obvious - if I can cause this much public venom, hatred and denunciation from big powerful market making firms, I must be doing something extremely right. Why the furor? What is it that can cause some of the most successful traders (market makers), traders utilizing billions of dollars in capital, traders having every conceivable advantage, traders who deal with every major institution, traders with research departments at their disposal, traders who have access to inside information (no, not them), traders with egos larger than life, to go off the deep end like this? What is it that can cause some of the highest profile Wall Street movers and shakers to conspire to defame, slander, impede and harass a small group of individuals who are merely trading small quantities of "high cap" Nasdaq securities at current quoted prices? It seems confusing but knowing the answer spells out big trouble ahead for them and unlimited opportunity for individual public day traders.

Day trading has been an honorable, rewarding, legitimate and envied activity since financial markets began trading. Wall Street professionals who participate in day trading activities such as dealers, speculators, traders, market makers, locals, floor traders and specialists are usually held in high regard and the successful participants are usually the subject of great admiration and envy.

The securities industry, however, and I mean all the securities marketplaces and exchanges (for stocks, bonds, commodities, options, etc.), has always chosen to have rules and regulations or physical restraints in place that put the public (investor/trader) at a significant disadvantage to the "Pro". Besides the spread (the difference between bid and ask prices), which is the most obvious disadvantage, poor access to the "real" market makes day trading almost impossible for the average person. Other obstacles include high commission costs (direct or indirect - see the discussion of payment for order flow in Chapter 10) and **access** to real time quotations and services (order execution).

Put all these obstacles together and the chances of succeeding as a day trader are slim to none.

Why would one want to be a day trader? Simply put, there is no activity more exciting, exhilarating, and potentially more rewarding than day trading. Day traders trade **flat** -- meaning they don't usually take home overnight positions in securities. Therefore, at 4:00 p.m. (the close of trading), their day is truly over - no worries or stress until the next day they wish to day trade. Weekends and holidays, they're off and their vacation is any time they choose to take it. Sure there is risk, intensity and stress during trading hours, but only during trading hours -- and boy do those hours go by quickly. Most of my associates curse long weekends because they love what they do so much. I truly believe the risk, intensity and stress is what makes trading so exhilarating and causes it to become almost addictive.

Unlike other professions, day trading gives one unlimited earnings potential. In addition, a day trader is usually held in high regard by his/her peers and envied for the career s/he's involved in. I would say a successful day trader is held in the same regard as other "professionals" such as doctors, lawyers, dentists, etc. I will not go into specifics about the earnings potential because this topic has been written about at arms' length in major, legitimate national publications (Time Magazine, Forbes, Business Week, Barrons, The New York Times) and I would be doing my associates and customers a disservice by going into too much detail. Besides, if I disclosed the results you probably wouldn't believe them anyway, thinking that my claims were similar to those on late night infomercials telling you to buy real estate with no money down. Suffice it to say many of my customers who were formerly unemployed or under-employed now park their fully paid for Mercedes in their fully paid for luxury home's garage. They certainly earn incomes, in many cases, equal to or better than those professionals I mentioned above. Sure there was a very small percent of losers, but they lost because they <u>stopped</u> day trading, lost their discipline **and,** for one reason or another, became "investors".

If you meet or think you meet the parameters set forth in this guide and follow the outlined strategies carefully, your probability of success will be exceptionally high. Whether you are male or female, young or old, black, white, brown or yellow, a high school dropout or Harvard graduate, you can very possibly become a very successful SOES trader. I have successfully trained machinists, beauticians, house painters, plumbers, bookkeepers, students, immigrants, retirees, doctors, lawyers, business owners and others to trade and make more money than they ever dreamed of. There are no defined criteria as to educational background or work experience.

Now let me make one thing perfectly clear --- I am not talking about day trading in a general sense. I am talking about day trading in **securities utilizing electronic execution, specifically SOES and SelectNet.**

My techniques utilizing SOES and SelectNet have been so successful for the past seven years that the market makers and the NASD have done everything in their power to reduce the effectiveness of and eliminate these systems. Why? Because these systems legitimize the way securities are traded, they level the playing field, and the last thing market makers want is legitimacy and fairness or a level playing field. They want an edge over you and the NASD has always allowed them to have it. As Tom Donlan stated in his editorial in Barron's, "After all, it is the National Association of Securities Dealers, not the National Association of Individual Traders". Until Now! Recent independent studies, SEC and Justice Department investigations and class action lawsuits naming almost every major market making firm have started to stem the tide of market maker abuse and open up day trading opportunities to everyone. The playing field in the stock trading arena is finally being leveled. Unlike other business opportunities, day trading requires no large illiquid capital investment. No up front buy-in money is required as there is in acquiring a franchise or other types of business ventures. Capital is needed for margin purposes only. Naturally, if you trade poorly your capital will be reduced. But day traders have their capital back at the end of every day plus or minus their profit or loss for the day. This phenomenon makes day trading a most attractive opportunity for the qualified individual.

How many businesses can one liquidate for cash at fair market value each and every day and re-enter whenever one chooses, if one chooses? What other business activity has unlimited upside but very controllable downside? What business activity can be expanded or reduced at will? What business activity has the well documented successful results of SOES Day Trading?

Day trading is **not** investing. It is a career opportunity. Your work is grinding out trading profits and the reward is unlimited earnings potential for the qualified individual. This guide will try to explain the criteria I believe necessary for success, including "personality types", capital requirements and all other relevant factors.

This book is basically a "how to" guide for day trading utilizing the advertised "market for the next 100 years". If you study its contents and decide day trading is for you, you will be in a position to prosper beyond your most optimistic expectations.

If you are unhappy in your current field of endeavor, this publication will expose a window of opportunity you might not have thought existed. If you are currently active in the market, you might well alter your approach to trading and learn to trade far more successfully while enjoying every minute of it.

CHAPTER TWO

WHAT IS SOES TRADING?

Trading has been around in a variety of forms since cavemen began bartering for goods and services. I will not elaborate on the history of trading because this is a guide to the future of trading, not its past.

People trade goods and services virtually every day of their lives. Most people call their trading a "job" where they trade their services (talents and skills) for monetary compensation. Others barter directly for other goods or services. The ability to trade astutely can make the difference between increasing or decreasing value received. This is ever so true in the day trading of financial instruments.

Numerous types of financial instruments are available for day trading. "Day trading" means that a security (any financial instrument) will be purchased and sold (or vice versa) within the same day -- and many times within minutes or even seconds. The objective of the day trader is to profit from short term swings in the price of the security being traded. Some examples of securities regularly day traded include stocks (listed on NYSE, AMEX, Nasdaq, etc.), bonds (traded on various exchanges as well as over-the-counter), options (listed on CBOE, AMEX, Pacific, PBE, etc.) and futures (on various futures exchanges), just to name a few.

A competent day trader really does not care what type of instrument s/he trades. To the day trader, all the various securities are merely an assortment of letters written on a trade ticket. It makes almost no difference what you trade as long as you trade it successfully. For example, a 1/2 point profit on 1000 shares of General Motors stock has the same profitability ($500 gross) as a 1/2 point profit on 1,000 shares of Apple Computer, 1/2 point on 100m IBM bonds, 1/2 point profit on 10 option contracts, 1/2 dollar profit on 10 gold futures contracts, 1/2 point profit on one US Treasury Bond futures contract, etc.

While it is true that it makes little difference what you trade as long as you trade it successfully, your ability to trade successfully can vary greatly depending on the arena in which you operate and how many impediments you face. The securities industry has spent many decades developing a system that gives innumerable advantages to the industry participants (Pros). For the individual day trader, unless s/he can also obtain certain of the advantages enjoyed by the industry, chances of success are minimal.

Some of the industry's advantages are quite obvious, while others, although very real, are barely noticeable. The biggest obvious advantage of the professional market maker, and obstacle to the day trader, is the "spread". The spread is the difference between the bid price (the price at which an individual can sell) and the offered or asked price (the price at which an individual can buy). The spread represents the market makers' reward for supposedly taking risk in a transaction. The fact that a market maker can buy a stock for a lower price and theoretically sell it at a higher price is the market maker's reward for absorbing the risk of price fluctuation. For example, the quoted share price of Apple Computer might be $46 bid while the offer might very well be a 1/4 point higher at $46 1/4. This means an individual trader buying and selling at the quoted market would be able to sell stock at $46 a share but would be required to pay $46 1/4 a share if s/he wished to purchase those very same shares. The 1/4 point difference is the "spread", representing the profit margin market makers hope to secure. A day trader has to first overcome the spread before a profit can be made. Spreads are present in virtually every type of financial instrument traded (stocks, bonds, futures, options, etc). Dealing with and analyzing spreads is discussed in Chapter 8.

The second major disadvantage to the day trader has been the lack of access to the "real market". The securities industry has continuously tried to keep real time quotes out of the hands of the general public. Even live business telecasts such as on CNN and CNBC display quotations delayed by 15 minutes. I never understood why these delays are permitted to exist. Once a trade report is released it becomes public news. That the media allows the news of a trade reported price to be delayed 15 minutes seems unconscionable; at least, it shows cooperation by the media to slow down dissemination of news, something the media would not do in the context of any other type of news. The knowledge of pricing cannot be delayed even for seconds if one hopes to compete in the day trading arena. Unless an individual is willing to commit to some relatively expensive quotation services, day trading is all but impossible. Most markets and exchanges also display quote changes and pricing information <u>after</u> they occur rather than showing market movements **while** they are happening. Why this phenomenon is of the utmost importance and how it affects you is discussed in Chapter 3.

The high cost of trading - "commissions" - is another impediment to day trading success. Despite massive amounts of advertising claiming extremely low commission rates for active traders - $10, $20, $25, $29 for any trade, any amount of shares; these advertisements are deceptive in that they do not disclose the true price you pay. They do not disclose that the broker is getting paid off by the "contra" (other) side of your trade, a practice known as payment for order flow - invariably costing you far more than the alleged discounted commission. The payoff received by <u>your</u> broker from the broker on the other side (the "contra") in many cases equals or exceeds the commission charges received from you. Who do you think they care about more? You or the firm paying them off perhaps millions of dollars annually? For example, you may be paying "only" a $20 commission on a trade of 1000 shares of stock, when in reality you very well might have been cheated out of 1/8 or 1/4 point on the price. The effects of payment for order flow are discussed at length Chapter 10.

Good access to your order entry person, the person who physically executes your orders, is another key factor. A successful day trader cannot tolerate any delay in the execution of his/her orders. Market makers (your real competitors) have immediate access to other market makers and can react in seconds to moving markets. A successful day trader must be able to do the same. As little as a second delay can cause you to miss a trade -- an almost insurmountable disadvantage.

Day trading using the techniques and technology I have been developing and utilizing for the past seven years has effectively removed all the disadvantages described above and enables the astute, disciplined trader to prosper far more than ever before imagined. I call this type of trading

"SOES TRADING"

The existence of the Small Order Execution System and SelectNet has eliminated significant advantages enjoyed for years by the market making community. They enable the average person to get an "honest" (as described by the head of the NASD himself), immediate, legitimate execution and to bid and offer shares in between the spread to achieve better prices. The individual day trader can now have his/her orders receive almost the same visibility as the market makers. Most importantly, it gives the individual the ability to have an order executed in a matter of 3-5 seconds.

SOES trading utilizing Nasdaq Level II quotes and SelectNet and Instinet information makes the average individual as well informed on prevailing market conditions as the market maker. It shows individuals "real" current prices as they are in the process of changing, allowing more astute decision making. In conjunction with a broker/dealer having SOES input ability; it allows access to the market and immediate entry into a fast moving situation. It puts you in control of the trading environment.

SOES trading could also be called informed trading. While our methods and techniques do not guarantee success, they most assuredly put all the tools necessary for success in your hands. The proof is of the pudding is in the eating. Most of my customers have enjoyed successes virtually unheard of in the trading community. These successes have been reported in Time Magazine (June 2, 1993), Barrons, Forbes and innumerable other prestigious publications.

A SOES trader is essentially a 21st century tape trader. How many times have you seen people sitting in a board room at a brokerage firm watching prices coming across a ticker tape? The ticker tape is the trader's primary source of trading ideas. As the symbols and prices float across the tape, occasionally someone will walk over to a broker and hand the broker an order based on something the client thinks s/he has identified on the tape. The broker will write up the order and pass it on to a teletype operator or other input staff person, who will then send it to the floor of the appropriate exchange or to a Nasdaq order entry clerk for execution. Hopefully, in a few minutes the customer will receive an execution showing the number of shares and price or a "nothing done", indicating the order did not get executed. This type of service is intolerable to the SOES trader. When a SOES trader gives an order to his/her order input person, s/he expects it to be completed within 5 seconds. This is the amount of time a typical order executed through SOES should take to be executed -- no if, ands or buts. The SOES trader, for better or worse, always has hands on control over his or her securities positions.

SOES trading involves intensive tape watching, but not in the conventional sense. Due to the rules of the Nasdaq market, all market makers in a particular stock electronically publish their current quotations on the Level II screen. Each quotation posted by a market making dealer in a Nasdaq stock must contain its bid price (the price at which it is willing to purchase shares), its offered price (the price at which it is willing to sell shares) and the minimum stated size (usually 1,000 shares) at which it must trade.

	AAPL $^{Security\ Symbol}$			
s*	GSCO	39 3/4	40 1/4	10x10
	Dealer Symbol	Bid Price	Offer Price	Size in Hundreds

*SOES Eligible

As dealers adjust their quotations, the new prices are

automatically displayed on the Nasdaq Level II screen. These changes are on-line and therefore displayed instantaneously. The SOES trader closely monitors these second to second price movements and interacts with them by buying or selling these shares while these stocks are still in the process of moving, while the trend is still intact - rather than after they have stopped or even paused. This is essentially the SOES strategy. The "trend is your friend" and a skilled tape watcher can benefit from an immediacy of execution if s/he can spot the trend developing early on.

I was totally amazed at how many experienced brokers working for major brokerage houses had never even seen a Nasdaq Level II screen. It seems like the real Nasdaq market is deliberately kept hidden from the typical broker. If the brokers are not allowed to see these quotations, how is it possible for the broker to look out for his/her customers? As the old saying goes, the major brokerage firms "treat their brokers like mushrooms - keep 'em in the dark and feed them a lot of sh--."

While other exchanges have order entry systems such as the "DOT" system on the NYSE, "AMEX" on the American Stock Exchange, and "MAX" on the Mid-West, these are order routing systems, that route or electronically direct the order to the appropriate specialist on the floor. While they work well, I have found that there are still too many idiosyncrasies and delays for my liking. The automatic execution of SOES affords a greater benefit to a trader. This, in conjunction with being able to possibly identify the emerging market trends in hundreds of Nasdaq stocks, is the mechanism of the SOES trading opportunity.

The typical SOES trader sits in front of a personal computer displaying Level II quotation services. This service is usually provided by the broker-dealer servicing the SOES trading customer at the offices of the brokerage firm; however, Level II service can be established in the individual trader's home or office. The on-site SOES trader usually has an added advantage by being in a "fertile" brokerage office where many ideas are exchanged, but much success has also been enjoyed by those operating outside of the broker-dealer office. Many traders feel they concentrate and focus better in the quieter environment of their home or office as opposed to the noisier although more "electrified" environment of an active brokerage firm. Another primary benefit of operating out of the broker's offices is the proximity of the SOES trader to the order execution personnel. Good proximity to the order clerk minimizes delays and potential errors. While a good idea can be worth many thousands of dollars, a productive environment, one in which is productive for you, can generate many good ideas. Only each individual knows for sure what kind of environment proves more productive for him or her. I discuss this proximity issue in Chapter 6.

SOES Traders Trade Nasdaq Listed Securities Only

There are hundreds of actively traded financial

instruments that are routinely traded every day. Why do we only trade Nasdaq listed securities? Simply because we have the greatest access to the market through SOES and SelectNet. It really doesn't make a difference what security it is that you trade, only that you trade it successfully by buying lower than you sell or selling higher than you buy. The most important difference is your ability to execute your transaction quickly and efficiently.

SOES and SelectNet do not guarantee profitability. They do guarantee that you will be able to interact in the market in an efficient and timely fashion. If you choose to buy you can do so immediately; if you want to sell you can do so immediately. SOES allows you to turn ideas into actions (consummated trades) and your actions into profits (or losses). SelectNet allows you to maximize your pricing in between the spread. You have the ability to advertise a better price to the entire marketplace - thereby allowing you the opportunity to make a little more or lose a little less. Remember, in day trading fractions count - they count a lot.

Another benefit of SOES trading is the virtually unlimited number and variety of different stocks that can be monitored for movement and therefore for trading opportunity. For example, a person involved in day trading a commodity such as gold or heating oil will be very disappointed or even bored if that particular commodity is not being actively traded on a particular day or time. Even if one is actually working on the floor of the commodity exchange itself, a dead day is a dead day. SOES trading, on the other hand, potentially involves monitoring hundreds of active Nasdaq stocks. With rare exception, there is almost always something going on somewhere in the Nasdaq market. The SOES trader goes to where the action is with the flick of a keystroke. It is unlikely that a commodities floor trader will run from pit to pit as easily as the SOES trader goes from stock to stock. There always seems to be a window of opportunity somewhere in the SOES environment. That's not to say one will always make money chasing this activity; however, the opportunity to profit almost always exists.

So, what is SOES trading? It is a way of operating in a very fertile environment where ideas become trades and trades become profits, where losses can be quickly cut and profits allowed to run. The ability to access markets within a few seconds assures the day trader that there is no need to delay the cutting of a loss -- you can always buy a stock back a minute later if you choose. Commissions are very low, so the cost of active trading is not burdensome. My typical customer trades about 40-80 times a day. That continued velocity and movement helps create a mindset that prevents significant loss while providing potentially tremendous trading profitability. SOES traders make their money by grinding out profits and cutting losses short. If you want to hit home runs, buy lottery tickets.

CHAPTER THREE

ADVANTAGES OF SOES TRADING OVER OTHER DAY TRADING

What makes SOES trading a better opportunity than other types of trading? Why have people who have never traded before had such tremendous success trading through SOES? The answer is quite simple - SOES levels the playing field for the individual trader. The elements present in SOES trading are unique to the financial markets. While other day trade opportunities exist, to my knowledge, only SOES trading combines use of the free flow of trading information and speedy execution. The availability of trade information and the ability to act on it is the essence of successful day trading. No matter what one trades on any exchange, success will depend on identifying opportunities via analysis of available information (both technical and fundamental), making a conclusion (a trade decision) and consummation of a transaction in the form of an executed trade.

It sounds quite simple, but transforming a good idea into consummated reality is very often a very difficult task. For example, there are numerous books on trading on option strategies - very often utilizing spreads. There are hundreds of "spread" ideas that are very valid and theoretically possible. However, putting on the spread (actually executing all sides of the transaction) at the desired prices is a much more difficult task. Frequently spreads cannot get executed within the theoretical parameters of the desired strategy. Floor brokers are usually charged with the setting up of spreads, and your ability to fine tune your situation is virtually nonexistent. This, many times, causes frustration levels to get very high. The quoted prices shown on the quotation services are not always accurate, specialists and market makers who are located on the trading floor "step" in front of your orders, and you as a customer are usually the last person to get serviced. Many times your "spreads" are executed only when no other "professional" wants them at that particular level.

Simply put, the current market structure gives the industry professional so many advantages that the individual trader is most assuredly at a statistical disadvantage. This is similar to one's chances in a gambling casino, where virtually every bet you make is at a statistical disadvantage to the house. For example, in the game of blackjack, even if you are an excellent player the odds will always be approximately 2% against you (49-51). This 2% will ultimately spell disaster if you play long enough. The casino knows this and relies on it to assure a relatively stable source of profitability based on overall handle. If you "card count" and gain a slight statistical edge, they will throw you out of the casino. Wall Street operates in a very similar way when dealing with active day traders.

Advantages of SOES trading over other types of day trading are as follows:

>Immediate access to the market
>Guaranteed liquidity
>Spotting market trends
>Shifting to an active arena
>Built-in discipline

<u>Immediate Access/Assured Execution</u> - Day trading on most exchanges usually involves delays in execution of 30 seconds to several minutes. Even orders executed through "automated" systems such as DOT (NYSE), AMEX (American Stock Exchange), MAX (Midwest), options market, commodities and others are not automated order <u>execution</u> systems; they are actually <u>routing</u> systems, meaning they quickly route your order to the specialist or market maker on the appropriate exchange for execution. Just because your order is quickly routed to the primary trading arena for that particular security is no guarantee that it will be executed at the quoted price you see on your quotation equipment. For any number of reasons, the trade you believe should be yours does not happen. Many times the quote is not accurate because of delays by reporters (exchange personnel who update quotes) in promptly adjusting markets (well, anyway, that's what they tell you). Other times they tell you the stock "traded ahead", meaning someone beat you to the punch. In some markets, they fail to give you the trade you believe you're entitled to because of a "fast market", which is usually

the biggest crock of all. Simply put, when markets are active or in the process of moving, getting satisfactory trade reports from most exchanges is a nightmare. If you have any experience in trading, I do not have to labor the point very much. Getting screwed on execution has almost always been the way it is.

Enter SOES. A system that essentially says "what you see is what you get" - quickly, efficiently, fairly and honestly. If the stock you see is quoted at a price and you are the first to access that price through SOES, it is yours - no stories, no excuses - just an executed trade and all within a few seconds. The system is impartial, legitimate, efficient, allows equal access for everyone and does not discriminate. It prevents market makers from "backing away" (failing to honor their market) and assures legitimate and liquid markets. The obvious result of this phenomenon is guaranteed liquidity for the SOES trader.

Guaranteed Liquidity - The fact that your orders (within SOES size/limitation) absolutely can be executed in seconds at the quoted market give the SOES trader assurances of guaranteed liquidity. Why is this so important? Primarily, because it enables the SOES trader to limit losses by being able to liquidate any unwanted positions in a matter of seconds regardless of how "busy" the market conditions are at the time the liquidation decision is made. As I discussed previously, and will emphasize continuously throughout this guide, cutting losses quickly is the key to trading success. In many other trading arenas it is not always possible to liquidate quickly, but in SOES trading it is routine. The peace of mind in knowing that you have hands on control over your losses is the single greatest advantage of the SOES system.

<u>Spotting Market Trends</u> - Utilizing the Nasdaq Level II market quotations in conjunction with SOES execution allows the astute SOES trader, in many instances, to see previews of coming attractions, in that one can, many times, identify an early trend in a stock while there is still in fact an opportunity to "get in" before the trend accelerates. By closely following market makers' price changes, an astute trader can many times observe a stock beginning to trend either up or down while still having time to access one of the remaining market makers before it has traded with someone else and has changed its price quotation. This enables the SOES trader to participate in the move while it is taking place. On other exchanges, the only basis for identifying a trend is by last sale price reporting, which tells you what <u>already</u> happened as opposed to what is in the process of happening. This is a subtle difference, but it can make the entire difference when day trading. Market makers, floor traders and "locals" all have a similar advantage on the listed equity, option and commodity exchanges. Now, for the first time, the SOES trader can enjoy inside "flow" information similar to the pros.

<u>Shifting to An Active Arena</u> - Unlike day trading in one specific type of security, SOES traders can readily shift to any arena (stock) they wish to almost instantly. Someone trading gold, for example, often is quite inactive at times when gold

is not moving around very much. Inactivity in the arena in which you trade does not present a profit opportunity. If there is no movement in the underlying security, it is virtually impossible to generate trading profits. Since there are literally thousands of NASDAQ stocks that trade every day, there are usually plenty of actively moving stocks that should meet the movement requirements of the SOES trader. For example, if Microsoft is trading in a narrow trading range, there might still be plenty of action in Apple, Lotus, Amgen, Intel or any of hundreds of other actively traded NASDAQ stocks. Each actively traded stock is an arena unto itself, and since there are hundreds to choose from, there is room for any number of SOES traders to be successful. No one need be crowded out. On many other exchanges, such as commodity futures exchanges, limited trading activity does not foster active participation by more than a few traders. If too many players enter the market, generating trading profits becomes almost impossible.

Nasdaq, because hundreds of issues are actively traded, provides the most opportune market for switching into fertile arenas.

<u>Built-in Discipline</u> - The SOES trader is limited as to the number of shares s/he can have executed for him through the SOES system with respect to any one order. At this writing that number in most cases is 1,000 shares. The limited size execution is for one transaction in the same security on the same side (buy or sell) during a 5 minute interval. After 5

minutes the SOES trader is free to execute another trade in that security on the same side.

This limited number of shares tradeable in one time period is large enough for most SOES traders to make a substantial trading profit, yet small enough to prevent a large loss if, in fact, the SOES trader maintains his/her discipline. SOES traders can increase their activities during busy times to the extent of their capital by diversifying in several stocks rather than maintaining a high concentration in one or two. This diversification spreads ultimate risk yet allows unlimited upside potential. So while the rule restrictions may sound a little unfair, they are really advantageous in that they build in a discipline factor of limited size.

All the above listed advantages make SOES trading, in my opinion, the greatest opportunity for any individual day trader trading any of the financial instruments available today.

CHAPTER FOUR

IS SOES TRADING FOR YOU?

Everyone I have spoken to about making money in Wall Street agrees on one thing - that they would like to make a lot of money - fast. Anything less than that is surely a compromise. If there were a sure fire way of achieving this goal, everyone would be rich, and therefore no one would be rich since "rich" is all relative.

In my 28 years in Wall Street, I have never witnessed a trading technique having the wide ranging success stories of SOES trading. During the seven years since I began using and training people in SOES trading techniques, I have had many success stories. Only a small percentage of would-be SOES traders failed; they did so because they stopped following the SOES trading techniques. The ones who follow the rules closely and do not hesitate have done exceptionally well. Some have become millionaires, others are making many times what they ever dreamed possible. My system is self-cleansing, meaning that, if you do not follow it you will probably lose money. If you do lose money, you may be required to deposit additional margin in your account in order to continue trading. At that point, if you choose not to continue, you can stop trading altogether or you can alter your trading techniques.

Not everyone has a personality suited for SOES

trading. Day trading requires certain personality traits that, while not uncommon, are not found in everyone. The fact that you are interested enough to read this publication gives me a good idea that you possess several of the needed qualities. Many of the characteristics of the successful SOES trader are interrelated, as you will see as I describe each one.

SELF CONFIDENCE - Trading is an art, not a science. In order to be a successful SOES trader, you must be confident that this system works and you must work the system with confidence. There is no assurance that any particular trade will work out successfully, but you must always have a true inner confidence in the belief that it works out on balance. This confidence keeps you going when you encounter a choppy day or are having a temporary losing streak. If you start to second guess your trading ability and lose your confidence in the system, chances of success are greatly diminished. I have used the SOES system for seven years. It works - the results are well documented. If you are confident enough and work the system according to the rules, you, too, will succeed.

While confidence is necessary, when confidence becomes arrogance or stubbornness it can be fatal in the SOES trading arena. If you are too confident (arrogant/stubborn) and do not quickly take your losses, you might very well get thrown out of the game (lose your capital). So while you need to be confident enough to make a decision quickly and act on it, you must also be confident enough to admit that you are wrong and reverse direction. If your confidence evolves into stubbornness or arrogance, you will be very sorry, very fast.

FOCUS - Trading is a very serious business. Large sums of money are made and lost every trading minute. The ability to stay focused on the essential elements of SOES trading is vital for success. Focus on the tape watching, order entry and position monitoring is uncompromising. Even a momentary loss of concentration can cost you hundreds or even thousands of dollars. The market continues to move whether you are watching or not. It does not stop because you go to lunch, the john or a coffee break. When you trade you must be able to stay focused on your task and keep distractions to a minimum. For example, if you get distracted and lose merely an 1/8 point on 1,000 shares of stock because you were late in getting in (or out), that represents a $125.00 loss. If it was 1/4 point, that loss is $250.00. A distraction of as little as 5 seconds can sometimes cause these problems. Focus is a must.

DISCIPLINE - Successful trading involves riding your winning transactions and cutting your losses short. Since winning transactions take care of themselves, the focus must always be on controlling the losses. That's where discipline comes in. If you are not disciplined, it will cost you lots of money. Losses hurt. People are very often reluctant to admit error and will not take a loss readily. <u>WRONG</u>. A successful trader, especially a SOES trader, must be disciplined enough to take the necessary actions quickly and without emotional distress. This trait is called Discipline. If you don't possess this trait, don't attempt SOES trading.

The people who attempted SOES trading and failed did so because they did not possess the necessary discipline to cut losses short. They allowed trades to get away from them to the point where they lost enough money to prevent them from continuing trading. To succeed at SOES trading you must continue to play the game (trade). If you are prevented from doing so because your capital is reduced too much, the game is over for you. You must have the discipline to cut losses quickly so the game is never over for you.

GOOD MEMORY - SOES trading is 21st century tape watching. You monitor the various market makers changing their quotes on Nasdaq Level II quotation equipment, check Selectnet and Instinet, try to identify trends and quickly act on your observations. This requires a good memory for changing stock prices and the ability to quickly recall and analyze the various brokerage firms quote changes. The better you can remember, recall and conclude, the more quickly you will be able to identify a trend and act on that trend. Since there are hundreds of stocks that potentially can be monitored and dozens of different market makers quoting them, a good memory is certainly a characteristic a SOES trader would want to possess.

AMBITION, HUNGER, DRIVE - SOES traders on balance are driven to succeed. They can taste the financial rewards of successful trading. SOES traders certainly are not passive. SOES traders crave winning and abhor losing. They love the "action" SOES trading provides. The intensity of the game and the possibility of high financial rewards make SOES trading exhilarating for the people who can handle intensity and exhilaration. SOES trading is not a game, it is serious work with large sums of money routinely changing hands. To participate effectively you must be ambitious, hungry and driven, whether you openly show it or are more controlled in appearance but still possess these qualities.

COMPETITIVE ATTITUDE - SOES trading involves head to head competition with market makers, institutions and the general public as well as with other SOES traders. It is perhaps the most competitive arena outside of professional sports. And as in professional sports, the results are known of at the end of the game (trading day). All the traits described previously are needed in order to put you in a position to compete. However, having these traits does not necessarily mean you have a competitive nature. The desire to win and succeed must be present if you wish to enter the SOES trading arena successfully.

CHAPTER FIVE

HOW HAVE OTHER SOES TRADERS FARED TO DATE?

SOES trading has been a life altering experience for almost everyone who has participated in it since its inception in 1988. With rare exception most of the SOES traders I have trained are making more money than they ever dreamed of and enjoying their new careers more than is imaginable.

I understand these claims sound really unbelievable, but the results are documented and have been reported on in such prestigious publications as Time Magazine, Business Week, Forbes and many others. The story of the SOES "Bandits" has been reported on television on such prominent shows as the Wall Street Journal Report, and on CNBC and even on the BBC (British Broadcasting Corp.) Most of my customers started with very little capital and a large amount of desire and discipline. If the success weren't real, why would the most powerful Nasdaq market making firms, the STA (Security Traders Association), and even the NASD itself be using every weapon in their arsenal to try to destroy the SOES system which the NASD developed? Why has the STA called SOES their "most pressing problem"? Their problem - your salvation.

I would love to give out actual results; however, due to the broker/client confidential relationship I cannot and will not do so. If, however, you do some further preliminary investigation I am sure specific representative earnings by typical SOES traders will not be hard to learn.

CHAPTER SIX

WHAT DO I NEED TO GET STARTED?

Assuming you've passed the personality, mental and emotional tests of the previous chapter, you are probably interested in knowing what else is required to enter this world of SOES trading. Simply put, there are three general elements that must secured in order to have the greatest chance of success. They are:

    1. Proper Basic Training.

    2. A Fertile Trading Location.

    3. Adequate Capital to Trade.

1. Proper Basic Training

As I discussed in the previous chapter, SOES trading is very competitive. The trading community does not feel compassion for newcomers and ease its competitive ways in order to give them a break. They would sooner chew you up and spit you out rather than allow you to take profits away from them. Therefore, before you begin trading you must be thoroughly familiar with all aspects of SOES trading. This guide will give you most of the theory behind SOES techniques; however, hands on training under the watchful eye of a SOES Pro is really a must before a novice gets into the trading arena. My experience with new candidates is that it takes approximately a month of observation and "paper" trading before the average candidate is ready to begin actual trading. Some people pick up more quickly, others take a while longer. Previous experience, market acumen, familiarity with computer screens, all either speed up or slow down the learning process. Thirty days is an average. If you rush and enter before you are ready, the trading community will have no problem in helping you "lighten your load" (taking your money). Your mistakes will be a welcome addition to their profitability.

Training begins first with observation and familiarization of the Nasdaq Level II quote equipment. There are several sources of this equipment including Nasdaq itself, PC Quote, Shark and Quotron, to name a few. Once familiar with the operation of your particular quotation service, you will be shown how to set it up for maximum utilization. Different formats are possible on most of the services and most traders vary the format slightly to suit their style.

Training continues with understanding Bid/Ask pricing, market maker recognition and reading the Nasdaq Level II tape. As you get more and more familiar with this data, you will quickly learn what the objectives are. At this point, getting comfortable with this fast moving data is essential. The objectives are quite obvious - buy low, sell high or sell high, buy low. As a new SOES trader observes trends developing, in a relatively short period of time s/he usually feels ready to jump in and trade. NOT YET! The neophyte should trade, but only "Paper Trade", meaning that s/he makes theoretical trades to see how they would have worked out.

"Paper Trading", however, is a far cry from real trading because the emotions do not kick in. It is an excellent training vehicle, but not totally realistic because real money is not on the line. The more seriously one tries to "paper trade", the more one will benefit from the experience.

Paper trading should continue for at least two weeks and be conducted as if it were real. Accounting for profit and loss should be performed in the same fashion as real trades. Do not fool yourself. Usually you get better results from paper trading than real trading. If you cannot paper trade successfully, it is very likely you will not trade successfully for real.

After observation and paper trading, the candidate will be eased into the real world. The candidate will open an account, deposit the necessary margin capital and be ready to proceed. At first the new trader will trade perhaps just one stock, either buying or selling short according to his or her sense of the prevailing trend. By watching just one stock, there is little distraction and the emotions of taking market risk can be felt. As the new trader becomes more comfortable with the machinery, his or her eye becomes trained to pick up the necessary changes and a sense of control develops. From this point on, the learning process accelerates exponentially because now the trader has money on the line. As proficiency develops, the SOES trader will grow to the extent his or her talent and capital allows.

MY STRONGEST SUGGESTION IS TO FIND A QUALIFIED SOES FIRM THAT HAS THE EXPERTISE AND IS EQUIPPED TO GIVE THE BEST HANDS ON TRAINING - IT WILL MAKE THE ENTIRE DIFFERENCE.

2. A Fertile Location

After the SOES trader has developed a degree of proficiency, his or her success to a great extent will be determined by the environment in which s/he operates. Some SOES traders choose to operate on their own out of their home or office in a distraction-free setting where they can concentrate on their trading. A speed dial set-up or direct wire must be set up to their executing broker, who must have made provisions to answer the SOES trader's calls immediately (and I do mean immediately). Any delay in a connection between the SOES trader and order executor usually will result in a "lost" trade (one that did not get executed or was executed at an inferior price). The delays caused by telephonically connected situations represent the biggest obstacle to the remote SOES trader. One solution is to maintain an open line to the order executing broker, but that is in practice very burdensome for the executing broker and can usually only be arranged for very active accounts that generate enough volume (commission) to compensate for that extra burden.

I have several clients who use this arrangement with good success. However, in my opinion, the best situation for the highest probability of success is for the SOES trader to be located at the offices of the executing firm. The advantages found at a well equipped SOES trading operation (for example, as in my firm, All-Tech Investment Group, Inc.) are quite numerous and very real.

Some advantages of a "fertile" (well equipped and properly thought out) SOES operation are:

>A) Direct communication (face to face) with your order input person. No outside telephonic communications are needed; there is no waiting for a telephone to be answered.

>B) Visual observation of your order being entered via a duplicate monitor of your order input person. This feature assures prompt entry and guarantees the accurate input of your exact instructions. You always have hands on knowledge of your exact situation - order entries, order cancellations, changes, etc.

>C) Sharing of ideas. A good idea can be worth thousands of dollars. If you sit at home or in your office you see only what you see. In a

"fertile" office environment the exchange of good ideas goes on all day long. You may very well pick up some good ideas by observing your fellow SOES traders in action.

Depending on the services provided at your SOES execution firm, there can be all sorts of information available to the astute SOES trader. Find out what the various SOES firms offer as to sources of good information. Good information and service will make the difference in your SOES results. What SOES firm you choose will be the most important factor in your SOES trading career.

3. Capital Needed.

Capital (the money needed to trade) is a lot like a baseball bat. It allows you to get up to the plate and swing (trade). A larger bat may allow you to hit farther, but sometimes it makes it so hard to swing that your batting average can fall off sharply. Especially in the early stages of your trading, you should not commit an excess of capital to more positions than you can monitor carefully or your ability to close out transactions at the optimal time will be compromised. On the other hand, if your bat (trading capital) is too small, you will be ineffective, it will break and you will strike out. Your bat (amount of trading capital) should be sized properly for the type of hitter (trader) you are.

Most people feel that to be effective in the investment

game you need a large amount of capital (money). This is very true -- if you are investing. SOES traders do not invest, they trade. They buy or sell relatively small amounts of stock and turn their positions frequently. Therefore you only need enough capital to meet the margin requirements of the relatively small number of positions you hold at any given time. As a position is closed out, the margin required for that holding is available for another trade. This rolling in and out of positions allows a relatively small amount of margin capital to go a very long way.

Your trading capital will either grow or shrink from trade to trade depending on how successfully you have been trading. For example, if you make a 1/4 point on a 1,000 share trade, your capital will increase by $250.00 less your commission charge. This increase is reflected immediately, and the additional capital is available immediately. However, likewise, if a 1/4 loss is experienced, your capital is immediately reduced by $250.00 plus the commission charge.

At this writing SOES trading is restricted to trading a maximum of 1,000 shares per trade. If the SOES maximum size limit is 1,000 shares you are still permitted to trade less than 1,000 shares if you wish to do so. Since 1,000 shares has proven to be a more optimally sized order, I will give you my opinion on the minimum required amounts of capital based on 1,000 share SOES trading.

In my SOES trading career I have trained many SOES traders. With the exception of a few, most started with a minimum capital base of $20-25,000.00. Because SOES trading has become a little more competitive and restrictive in the past few years, the need for capital, in my opinion, has increased somewhat. As a general rule, a SOES trader should have at least $50-100,000.00 of risk capital available to commit to trading. This should be <u>risk</u> capital, money that, if lost, will not devastate one's financial life. While many customers have had tremendous success starting with less, the $50-100,000.00 range should allow adequate capital for enough flexibility to trade effectively. If the new SOES trader experiences a little difficulty or a slow start, there will be enough excess to cover a rocky beginning.

One of the beautiful things about SOES trading is that if, for some reason, you do not do well and your capital is reduced, you <u>must</u> replenish it or you will be precluded from continuing to trade. This is a fail safe mechanism in that if you decide to stop, a good part of your capital should still remain even if you decide to call it quits. Other types of endeavors frequently result in the entire loss of your risk capital. In SOES trading your capital is always liquid and available to you (plus or minus your trading profit and loss). While you put your capital at risk, the risk is only as great as <u>you</u> make it. You assume market risk (trading risk), not capital investment risk.

CHAPTER SEVEN

CHOOSING YOUR SOES FIRM

You think you meet all the requirements set forth in the previous chapters. You've explored other business opportunities and realize SOES trading might possess the best potential of any of your alternatives. You have the personality, capital and desire. You want to get started. You ask yourself: "How do I find a brokerage firm that can get me started? One that can properly train me, set me up with the necessary equipment and provide me with the services I need to succeed?" Good questions.

Unfortunately the NASD, at the urging of the powerful market maker interests, has made being a "SOES" firm very difficult. The NASD continuously harasses the SOES firms in an effort to stifle their proliferation. While an entire book can be written on this issue (and probably will be), suffice it to say that finding an accommodating, teaching and fertile SOES firm is probably the most difficult part of SOES trading. You should choose a firm that can spend the necessary time to teach you and set you up in an environment that will give you the highest probability of success, a firm that has a fertile environment where ideas flow freely.

As the original "SOES Bandit", a term I now find endearing, I believe the firm I developed, All-Tech Investment Group, Inc., meets these needs. There may be a few other organizations, most of which have their origins traced back to All-Tech, but most do not provide the broad based elements required for successful SOES trading. While most can execute orders, they lack any teaching acumen. More importantly, most do not provide the fertile environment - one in which good trading ideas abound.

When choosing a SOES firm, look for one that fits your personality and has patience with the new trader or non-experienced customer. SOES trading is very competitive. More experienced customers have little tolerance for novices who slow up order entry or make verbal errors. The new SOES trader must learn the "language" of trading. The firm you work through must be tolerant and accommodating. Commission rates on a per trade basis are very low and there is absolutely no room for errors. The pace is fast and sometimes tempers are short and intensity runs high. A good SOES firm understands this and takes novices under its wing and stays with them until they are capable of interacting properly with the more experienced SOES traders.

All-Tech Investment Group, Inc. has been training and developing the most successful SOES traders in the industry since 1988. The bulk of the SOES trading firms now in existence trace at least part of their origins back to All-Tech. All-Tech has been the primary defender of SOES rights and has spent millions of dollars on the defense and perpetuation of SOES and all electronic execution services. All-Tech's efforts have laid the groundwork for the significant changes that are now being made and will be made in the future to the Nasdaq market. We are very proud of our efforts and results.

While we probably could not accommodate every potential SOES trader, we are best equipped to analyze your needs and potential and if necessary refer you to other SOES active firms based on your geographic, technical and logistical requirements.

Remember - affiliating oneself with the proper SOES firm will be the single most important step in being a successful SOES trader.

CHAPTER EIGHT

SOES TRADING TECHNIQUES

You've done it! You've found the right firm, set up your account, learned how to use the various quotation equipment, understand how to enter and change orders and feel ready to begin. Now what? What trading technique (style) will you employ? Although from the outside most SOES trading looks the same, subtle differences exist in every trader's style. Basically, all you do is identify a trend, enter, wait for the anticipated move to occur, and then close out accordingly. Seems simple and basic, but within this "simple" scenario are many possible variations, variations that can make major differences in your profitability. There are several techniques you can employ; all will work with varying degrees of success. The most important thing is to be consistent with whatever style you choose, rather than continually changing.

<u>Grinding</u> - Many traders, the ones I believe do best, employ a low tolerance, high velocity (LTHV) trading style. This means they get in and out of their positions very quickly and have a very low tolerance for loss. These traders watch many actively traded stocks, get in quickly on seeing a trend developing, grab a quick 1/8 or 1/4 point and say goodbye. If they cannot get an 1/8, a 1/16 will suffice. If even that does not come and the trend appears to be reversing, they will sell out flat or even at a small loss almost immediately. They realize one thing: stocks do not "wear out"; you can trade

them over and over again and they remain the same. Losses are totally unacceptable to the LTHV trader. If the LTHV trader gets out too soon, s/he can reenter once again; the "trend must remain their friend." This style requires constant focus and attention. This is also called "grinding" because the trader is continuously grinding out profits 1/8 by 1/8 and 1/4 by 1/4. This technique generates many transactions and total commission costs are higher than with other techniques; however, in my experience the "grinders" have had the greatest overall success with the least amount of real exposure. The LTHV trader seldom reads business newspapers such as The Wall Street Journal or Investors Business Daily, or listens to financial news reports. The LTHV trader's sole reason for making a trade is price movement. S/he does not care why a stock is moving, only that it is moving. S/he does not analyze stocks or care about fundamentals - only short term price movements. The LTHV trader goes with the flow and maintains no opinions. This may seem easy, but if one possesses the other traits necessary for SOES trading, it may be very difficult to "have no opinion." Finally, the "grinder" virtually never takes home an overnight position.

<u>Specialists</u> - This group of SOES traders "specializes" in a handful of very actively traded stocks and concentrates only on as few as 5-10 stocks. The stocks they will trade, such as Microsoft, Apple, Lotus, US Healthcare, Intel, etc., are the most active of the most active stocks. They develop a "feel" for these securities and utilize SOES and SelectNet

to enter and exit them freely. Since these securities almost always have significant intraday moves, there is plenty of opportunity to catch swings. In many cases "specialists" work in teams (more than one together) so they never miss even a small blip. This intense concentration on relatively few stocks gives them confidence that a situation will never "get away" from them because of an oversight. Specialists make extraordinarily good money by sometimes "pressing" their positions; that is increasing them to more than one lot (1,000) as the trend continues in their favor (within the restrictions of SOES regulations). Risk is minimal for "specialists" because they have a handle on all their positions at all times. The novice SOES trader is best advised to start as a "specialist" before venturing into the "grinding" arena. Those who do not have the "head" (extensive memory) for grinding are best advised to play the SOES trading game as a "specialist". Very handsome profitability has been generated by my clients acting as "specialists". The specialist usually knows a little more about the stocks s/he trades but not so much as to develop a strong opinion. The most important information the know is when earnings are to be announced and other relevant information that might cause a price movement at a particular time. Fundamental analysis is not very important and should almost always be avoided.

Parameter Traders - The parameter traders are similar to the grinders except that instead of jumping in and out of a stock very quickly, they allow for larger interim moves (both for them and against them) but within a disciplined parameter.

For example, if they buy a stock and it does not go up immediately or declines slightly, they may stick with it for a while, but within a predetermined parameter (perhaps 1/2 point). If the stock continues down to where the loss is 1/2 point, it is then immediately liquidated. On the other hand, if it goes up, they will usually hold a little longer to maximize profitability. It is not sold out for the first 1/8 or 1/4 profit, but rather held for the potentially larger profit. The benefit of this technique is that you do not get "chewed up" by a choppy market. Your tolerance for a little more "pain" can help avoid the continuous buying and selling a stagnant, choppy market can create. This technique can also save a little in commission charges, but if the parameters are not part of a strict discipline, large losses will occur. Only the most disciplined SOES trader should employ a parameter strategy. It is useful for the SOES trader who is a little more "laid back" in his approach and cannot readily handle a "grinder" or "specialist" approach.

Sharp Shooter - A sharp shooter is someone very patient who methodically watches the tape and screen, entering only when s/he is "absolutely" sure a good trading opportunity exists. Unfortunately, being absolutely sure is far from absolute. Because stocks usually look best at the top and worst at the bottom, "sharp shooting" is very difficult. SOES traders sometimes become "sharp shooters" when they are in a slump, thinking that by trading more slowly and deliberately they will do better. The fact is they usually don't. SOES traders usually try getting into a "rhythm" with the market and flowing with it. The "trend is your friend" is the attitude most SOES traders live by. While being methodical and cautious are good traits, if being overly so takes you out of the flow, if it keeps you from "pulling the trigger" and participating in the trend, then it could be causing more harm than good.

Since nobody knows which trend will be real and extended, the SOES trader will many times get "jiggled" in and out of a stock. This is part of the game and there is no way to prevent the small losses created by "jiggles". They are irritating as hell, but an integral part of SOES trading. Without jiggles and some losses, everyone would make money on every trade, therefore everyone would be a SOES trader and therefore there would be no game at all. Thank goodness for losses!

<u>Diversion Trader</u> - A "diversion trader" is someone who loves the action of trading, but has another rewarding full time profession or is perhaps retired. Businessmen, doctors, lawyers, engineers, etc. are often bored with the routine of their professions. They use SOES trading as a "diversion" from their regular career activities. Since SOES trading is very short term in its nature, anyone can participate for even a short period during the day. The excitement and intensity invigorates these SOES traders and usually they find it a wonderful diversion from their everyday world. All they need is Level II quotation service and a speed dialer and they are all set to participate in this exciting arena. Usually these

SOES traders stay in the most volatile, actively traded stocks so they can participate in the action and get the moves they seek in short periods of time during the day. Their styles vary and SOES trading is done as much for the enjoyment of trading as it is for gain.

<u>Occasional Windfalls</u> - The nature of the SOES trading business is such that on average about once a month, or at least bi-monthly, there is an unusually large, intraday move in an active SOES stock. An active SOES stock (see list), one very often traded by the majority of SOES traders (<u>e.g.</u>, Apple, Microsoft, Intel, Lotus), can on occasion have news or be subject to takeover speculation and move several points in a matter of minutes. The astute trader utilizing almost any style will jump in on these situations and usual make a "windfall profit". For example, in February 1995 shares of AMGEN started to move up from $65 a share. Amgen started to climb quickly and steadily eighth by eighth to as high as $76, all in a matter of 15 minutes. Most SOES traders were involved by the time the stock reached $68 and out between $75 1/2 and $74 3/4 as the stock began to correct lower. This 10 point move on millions of shares in volume was a result of takeover speculation and enabled the SOES trader to take a 6-10 point profit in a matter of minutes. Based on a mere 500 share position, this translated into a $3,000-$5,000 profit.

Although phenomena like this do not occur on a daily or weekly basis, they do occur on average about 6-10 times a year and are a real shot in the arm to the SOES trader. While most career SOES traders do not count on these windfalls, they do occur fairly often and are very instrumental in significantly increasing the annual income of the SOES trader. A "fertile" trading environment is the most important factor in making sure one participates and does not miss the windfall trades. In the fertile environment, many SOES traders work in close proximity and many eyes are monitoring stocks. If one "breaks out" it is usually spotted by someone who passes along the information, thereby allowing everyone who wants to participate to do so. SOES traders working on their own might miss this action because they very well might not be monitoring that particular stock. As they say on Wall Street, "a good idea can be worth a lot of money."

Another source of "windfall profits", but to a smaller extent, is "crossed markets". A crossed market is one where, simultaneously, market makers are bidding for shares at a higher price than other market makers are offering them. For example, one or more market makers might be bidding $40 a share for Apple, while at the same time, other market makers are offering shares for sale at $39 1/2. This happens occasionally in active markets, when news comes out, on the opening of trading and for various other reasons. Market makers are not supposed to cross markets, but they do so on occasion and this creates a windfall scenario for the quick thinking SOES trader. The reason the NASD allows for trades to be executed on crossed markets is to give market makers the "economic incentive" to keep their markets in line.

By SOES trading on crossed markets you are actually doing the market a service by arbitraging the market and keeping it orderly. Thank you! If you locked in virtually riskless profits, that is your reward for your help in keeping the markets honest and orderly.

CHAPTER NINE

SPOTTING MARKET TRENDS

Throughout this guide I have talked about identifying or spotting market trends and quickly acting on them. This is at the heart of SOES trading and profitability. But how does one really know or at least have the highest probability of spotting and identifying a "real" trend as opposed to just another market "jiggle"? This is often the toughest question of all.

Perhaps the best or at least the most often used factor in analyzing a move is to check out "who", meaning which market makers, are moving their quotations. Certain market makers are more of a factor in the stocks they trade than others. The market makers that seem to be the biggest factors in a stock are usually the firms with the largest institutional clientele. Firms like Goldman Sachs, Salomon, First Boston, Morgan Stanley and Merrill Lynch handle a great deal of large institutional order flow and are more likely to be "real" in a stock. Being "real" is a way of describing the probability that they will usually stay at a quoted price and trade rather than run away from their quoted market. These dealers many times have large orders in the stocks they trade which make their markets "real" or they at times will commit a good deal of "firm" capital to a position when trading a stock.

Contrarily, many market making firms very rarely desire

to hold positions or commit firm capital and only look to get a piece of the action on a large volume of retail orders (known as getting in between orders). These firms get their orders by giving payoffs to retail firms and quickly flipping the shares to anyone for small fractional profits. Firms such as Mayer & Schweitzer, Herzog, Troster, Nash Weiss, etc. are known as trade houses and are often real only if they have an order in hand. They seldom commit capital to position trading and are not real factors in pricing (without an order in hand). They trade for the spread.

Then there is the "Ax" in a stock. The Ax is a firm that has a particularly large interest in a specific stock. Sometimes it was an underwriter in the shares, has a big research coverage, or has a big retail interest in the stock. For example, Piper Jaffray, for years, has been an Ax in the shares of St. Jude Medical. A SOES trader should pay extra attention to Piper's price movements when entering into trades of St. Jude. The fact that a particular firm in a stock is the Ax, however, does not always mean its pricing is indicative of the apparent direction of the trend. In fact, since they often have many buyers and sellers, these firms often "fade" the trend - meaning they sell into an up trend and buy into a down trend. It is, however, very important to monitor the "Ax" in a stock and be aware of its actions. The Ax many times can stop and/or reverse a trend. In order to find out who the Ax is in a stock you can check to as to who did their latest secondary, is their investment banker, has research coverage or owns an inside piece of stock. More simply, if you are in a fertile environment, just ask someone who has been following the stock - 9 out of 10 times they will know.

The spread cutting firms are a new breed of market makers interested in competitive markets and profiting from trading by competing in between the historically large NASDAQ spreads. They are hated by most other market makers for "breaking spreads", but are very often the best indicator of price movements because their markets are usually real, though not necessarily sizeable. If a spread cutting firm moves, it is usually because they bought or sold shares at their previously quoted level. They do not often play games with their pricing and trade based on supply/demand factors. Domestic Securities, Inc.(DOMS) is one of a very few (if any) spread cutting firms. I am proud to be the president of DOMS and hope to make truly competitive markets a reality for the betterment of the SOES trader as well as financial markets in general.

CHAPTER TEN

WIGGLES, JIGGLES & HEADFAKES

When I first started to utilize SOES for trading back in 1988, it was relatively easy to spot trends, enter quickly and exit profitably. Only myself and a few traders represented the entire "SOES TRADING" community, market makers' minimum SOES exposure (the amount of shares any individual market maker had to honor) was 5,000 shares. There was no short sale rule or any other restrictive regulations and competition between SOES traders was virtually nil. Today things have changed and it is generally more difficult to SOES trade now than in 1988.

At the urging of the major market marking firms, the NASD has passed numerous discriminatory rules and regulations in an attempt to eliminate the SOES traders from marketplace. Since 1988 I have been the primary advocate fighting for the rights of the SOES traders. This battle, which continues to rage to this very day, has cost millions of dollars in legal fees, time and effort, but recently we have had some long awaited success. This success is paving the way for more SOES traders to enter the market. Having more SOES trading participants will ultimately lead to the phenomenon of more "wiggles, jiggles and headfakes".

Market makers have become much more experienced in dealing with SOES traders. At first market makers very often overreacted to a flurry of buy and sell orders from the SOES traders. Now market makers realize that the actions of SOES traders are overall net neutral to the marketplace; SOES traders buy and sell virtually the some numbers of shares daily and the net activity should not move the markets. This realization has created many more "wiggles and jiggles" in the intraday price movement of SOES stocks. For example, when several SOES traders decide to buy APPLE at a certain point in time, several market makers might move up their quotations as they each sold a small quantity of shares. Other market makers move their price quotation just because they saw other market makers moving, without even making a print (trade at their quoted level). Market makers have begun to realize that when SOES traders come in to buy shares, it is only a matter of time (usually only a very short period) until they will be offering to sell back those very same shares. Therefore, now we see that several more astute market makers are starting to "fade the trend" (selling into the SOES buyers) and then downticking the stock, causing SOES traders to panic and sell out. This type of action creates what I call "wiggles and jiggles". Stocks go up (or down) a small amount, stop and reverse - sometimes several times a day. This type of action drives a SOES trader nuts. Because SOES traders must overcome the spread and expenses (commissions), wiggles and jiggles cost them dearly and have the greatest negative influence on profitability.

Since it is almost impossible to know for sure whether a perceived move is "real" and/or the beginning of a significant trend or just a jiggle, the SOES trader must act on his/her best judgment and hope for the best. If you get "jiggled" out, so be it. Persistency and discipline must always be maintained. There will be days when you get wiggled and jiggled like crazy, but that is a reality and a cost of doing business. On balance this reality, if handled with good business sense, can be kept under control and does not deter the successful SOES trader. The overall advantages of SOES trading significantly outweigh the difficulties created by the wiggles and jiggles.

"Headfakes" are a problem similar to wiggles and jiggles. Whereas wiggles and jiggles are created by routine market maker actions that have come about through their increasing experience in dealing with SOES traders, "headfakes" seem to be more deliberate. "Headfakes" are movements by a market maker or market makers (sometimes in concert) designed to create an illusion to induce market participants and the SOES trading community to take an action (i.e., buy or sell). For example, if a market maker wants to create selling (they are really a buyer), they would try to give the illusion of weakness by having a few of their market making "friends" initiate a downtick at about the same time. This gives an "illusion" of weakness and there is a good chance several SOES traders would be induced to sell shares into this staged decline. After the selling is completed, these conspiring market makers would quickly reverse the trend and "catch" the SOES traders. Often head faking occurs around lunchtime. Lunch hour headfakes appear to be a game created to amuse market makers during a time of day when very little activity may be occurring in the markets. Of course, market makers vehemently deny that they conspire to fix quotes or spreads, but most observers who follow these markets know better. Anyway, the U.S. Department of Justice and the Securities and Exchange Commission (SEC) are investigating collusion by market makers and their conclusions will be known in the near future. Headfakes can be costly, but once again, just as in the wiggles and jiggles scenario, they are part of the business and overall do not have to be a significant negative in your SOES trading career.

To lessen the affects of wiggles, jiggles and headfakes, most SOES traders try to trade only stocks that are very active with a relatively large float and capitalization. "Active large cap" stocks, as they are known, such as INTEL, MICROSOFT, APPLE, LOTUS, US HEALTHCARE, etc., are much more difficult to wiggle and jiggle. They trade so actively and there is so much institutional interest that it is very difficult for a market maker to move them around or create any false illusions.

Recent allegations by reputable professors at well known universities of collusion to fix spreads in the Nasdaq markets have helped to narrow spreads in several "active, high cap" SOES stocks in recent months. Professors Shultz and Christie's report alleging collusion among market makers has been the catalyst for numerous class action lawsuits and the Justice Department and SEC investigations. I am proud to be working along with these government officials on behalf of the public investing and trading community. Hopefully, the new awareness of what is going on will help to level the playing field for all market participants. If the market making community realizes that the regulators will not tolerate improper and illegal behavior and collusion, the markets will become more legitimate and the small guy will have more confidence and a far better chance to succeed.

So far these investigations and lawsuits have resulted primarily in the reduction of spreads in a few of the largest and most actively traded Nasdaq stocks. In the past few months, the spreads on such key stocks as INTEL, APPLE, LOTUS, SUN MICROSYSTEMS, CISCO SYSTEMS, ORACLE SYSTEMS, DIGITAL and others has been reduced to an 1/8 point from either 1/4 or 1/2 point spread previously. This spread reduction has reduced the spread exposure on these stocks and therefore reduced the risk and increased the potential rewards to the SOES trader. As more and more competition is permitted in the marketplace, tighter spreads and more legitimate markets will most assuredly be enjoyed by other stocks.

Hopefully another result of the investigations will be the end of the practice of "payment for order flow". In this practice market makers pay off the order entry firms (your broker) to show the orders they have (including yours) to them. Supposedly they give you a competitive price, but the reality is you wind up getting the worst "legally" acceptable price permitted, meaning that the customer receives the best price quoted on Nasdaq. This in no way assures you the "best" price, only the best price on Nasdaq. More advantageous prices are generally available on other systems (Instinet, SelectNet, Midwest Stock Exchange, etc.), but your broker has absolutely no incentive to find them for you, despite the fact that the broker's duty is to work in your best interest. After all, why should your broker give up the 2 or 3 cents a share the broker is getting paid from the market makers' payoff and maybe have to spend a penny or two to get you the better price on one of the automated systems. The brokers who accept payoff for orders violate their fiduciary obligation to you, their client. Nobody who understands the underlying corruption of payment for order flow would deal with a broker who accepts it. Yet, virtually every discount broker accepts these payments in the ordinary course of its business. These payments raise the real cost to you of the trade, in many cases far above the stated commission rates.

It is virtually impossible for a SOES trader to operate his/her business through a firm that accepts payment for order flow. These firms virtually never use the SOES for immediate order execution or SelectNet for bidding or offering your shares in between the spread. Some even have house rules against it. The discount broker depends on these payoffs to survive and "best" execution takes a back seat to the broker's own profitability. When regulators finally decide to outlaw this practice, the markets will truly become more competitive and spreads will dramatically narrow.

CHAPTER ELEVEN

EVALUATING THE MARKET MAKERS

What separates the men from the boys in the SOES trading arena? Why do some people do well while others do extremely well? Some say its instinct, others say focus and still others luck. I say it is all of the above but that skill is most important. The skill that develops upon being able to read the ticker tape and really understand what it is telling you.

The changing numbers alone do not tell the whole story. While you might think you have identified a trend by seeing many price changes in a particular stock, the highly skilled trader might see an entirely different scenario. The experienced, skilled SOES trader is familiar with not only identifying price movements, but is also very knowledgeable about "who" is making those price movements. Distinguishing between the multitude of market makers who change their prices and analyzing what the changes mean is a skill that separates the men from the boys (and women from girls).

All market makers are not created equal. As the SOES trader soon learns, being able to differentiate between the significant market makers and the market makers who just go along for the ride is a skill that must be developed. The fact is that most market makers are not very interested in making markets and taking risk. In all too many cases, a market maker is in a particular stock only in the hope of "catching an order", an order it can trade against. What I mean by "trading against" is that the market maker will quote a price for a stock based only on the premise that it can turn around and fill an order it already has in hand - risklessly. If the market maker has a buy order, it can buy stock against that order knowing it can always sell that stock to its buyer - risklessly. Alternatively, if the market maker has a sell order, it can offer stock "short" knowing it can buy the stock back from the seller - risklessly. It's a "no brainer" and almost always profitable. These market makers have no desire to position stocks (keep an inventory) and are only a factor in a particular stock when they have an order. Their influence is temporary and they very seldom quote the inside market.

Other market makers, though few in number, are the movers and shakers in the Nasdaq market. These firms usually handle many institutional orders and commit significant capital to the positioning of various stocks. They are many times called the "Ax" in the stock. If not the Ax, they are at least "real" market makers. The SOES trader soon learns to respect their movements and pay attention to their actions. I do not believe there are more than a dozen market making firms that meet this criterion. While many firms are the Ax in a stock from time to time, very few have significant influence on SOES stocks (stocks often traded by SOES traders) on a continuous basis. SOES stocks are usually the better capitalized, actively traded, higher priced Nasdaq stocks (Microsoft, Intel, Apple, Lotus, etc.). The "real" market makers usually trade all of these stocks and seem to have orders in hand or an inclination to heavily position these shares at all times. You can assume that they will not run for the hills when a few small orders come their way.

Who are the market makers? How do they differ? Who exercises power and who runs away? Your ability to answer these questions will ultimately determine how successful you become in your SOES trading career. To help you get started and give you the best chances not to make obvious mistakes, I have surveyed a group of seasoned SOES traders and asked them to give me on a 1 to 10 basis their evaluation of the primary market makers in SOES stocks.

This survey asked the respondents to analyze the overall significance of the individual market maker as related to their market moving potential, perceived sizeability, influence in moving other market makers, willingness to trade at their quoted prices and general leadership in the stock. Ten indicates the highest respect for a market makers markets and movements while a 1 indicates it is perceived as a meaningless factor in the pricing or movement of the particular stock. Only one firm received almost a unanimous 10 rating. It is no surprise to most SOES traders that this honor goes to Goldman Sachs, a fine firm that honors its markets and is the undisputed champion of market making as viewed by the SOES trading community and probably most other market watchers. Following behind Goldman and also highly rated by the survey were Merrill Lynch, First Boston and Morgan Stanley. While a few other market makers received respectable scores, the above firms were the ones that seemed to have the most impact in influencing trading decisions by SOES traders.

Naturally, almost all of the survey's candidates can be and are significant players in particular stocks at specific times; however, the market makers named above seem to exert influence on an ongoing basis. Knowing where they are at all times is a good policy to follow.

The chart below analyzes 68 of the market makers most often found trading the most popular SOES stocks. Remember, the higher the evaluation (10 being the maximum), the greater the perceived influence of the market makers. A low score (1 being the minimum) indicates little respect for a market maker's influence over price movement in the stock.

MARKET MAKER	SYMBOL	AVG SCORE	MY EVAL	HI/LO FROM SURVEY
ALEX BROWN & SONS INC.	ABSB	7	7	6-8
AEGIS CAPITAL CORP.	AGIS	4.37	4	1-6
BEAR STEARNS & CO., INC.	BEST	6.34	7	5-8
BT SECURITIES CORP.	BTSC	3.50	4	2-6
CANTOR FITZGERALD & CO., INC	CANT	5.64	6	4-7
CHICAGO CORPORATION	CHGO	4.64	4	3-7
CJ LAWRENCE/DEUTSCHE BANK	CJDB	3.12	5	1-5
CARLIN EQUITIES CORP	CLYN	2.19	3	1-5
COASTAL SECURITIES LTD	COST	3.91	5	1-7
COWEN & CO.	COWN	6.19	7	4-8
DAIN, BOSWORTH INC.	DAIN	4.09	5	2-6
DEAN WITTER REYNOLDS	DEAN	4.91	6	2-6
DONALDSON, LUFKIN & JENRETTE	DLJP	4.46	4	2-6
DOMESTIC SECURITIES INC.	DOMS	5.09	7	3-8

MARKET MAKER	SYMBOL	AVG SCORE	MY EVAL	HI/LO FROM SURVEY
EXPONENTIAL CAPITAL MARKETS	EXPO	2.40	3	1-6
FIRST ALBANY CORP.	FACT	3.46	4	1-7
FAHNESTOCK & CO., INC.	FAHN	3.46	4	1-7
FIRST BOSTON CORP.	FBCO	7.50	8	5-9
FOX-PITT, KELTON INC.	FPKI	5.28	4	3-7
GRUNTAL & CO. INC.	GRUN	4.19	4	2-6
GOLDMAN SACHS & CO.	GSCO	9.75	10	8-10
GVR CO.	GVRC	3.28	3	2-6
HAMBRECHT & QUIST INC.	HMQT	5.91	7	3-8
HERZOG, HEINE, GEDULD INC.	HRZG	6.34	7	5-9
JEFFERIES CO. INC.	JEFF	5.55	6	2-7
J.P. MORGAN SECURITIES INC.	JPMS	5.91	6	4-7
KEMPER SECURITIES INC.	KEMP	3.28	4	1-6
LEHMAN BROTHERS INC.	LEHM	6.84	8	4-9

MARKET MAKER	SYMBOL	AVG SCORE	MY EVAL	HI/LO FROM SURVEY
BERNARD MADOFF	MADF	3.73	3	1-7
MAYER & SCHWEITZER, INC.	MASH	6.64	7	4-8
M.H. MEYERSON & CO., INC.	MHMY	5.42	5	4-6
MERRILL LYNCH	MLCO	7.84	8	6-10
MONTGOMERY SECURITIES	MONT	6.82	7	5-8
MORGAN STANLEY & CO., INC.	MSCO	8.42	9	6-10
MIDWEST STOCK EXCHANGE	MSWE	4.37	3	2-8
NASH WEISS & CO.	NAWE	4.64	4	2-7
NEEDHAM & CO. INC.	NEED	5.37	5	3-7
NOMURA SECURITIES INT'L INC	NMRA	3.28	3	1-5
OLDE DISCOUNT CORP.	OLDE	5.28	5	2-7
OPPENHEIMER & CO. INC.	OPCO	5.67	6	2-8
PERSHING TRADING COMPANY	PERT	3.37	5	1-6
PIPER JAFFRAY INC.	PIPR	6.09	7	4-7

MARKET MAKER	SYMBOL	AVG SCORE	MY EVAL	HI/LO FROM SURVEY
PRUDENTIAL SECURITIES INC.	PRUS	6.34	7	4-9
PUNK ZIEGEL & KNOELL INC.	PUNK	4.34	5	2-7
PAINE WEBBER INC.	PWJC	6.55	8	5-8
RAGEN MCKENZIE INC.	RAGN	3.40	4	1-6
RAUSCHER PIERCE REFSNES INC.	RPSC	5.73	7	4-8
ROBERTSON STEPHENS & CO. LP	RSSF	5.37	5	4-7
SALOMON BROTHERS INC.	SALB	6.82	8	4-8
SANDS BROTHERS & CO. LTD	SBNY	4.25	4	1-7
SMITH BARNEY SHEARSON INC.	SBSH	7.09	8	5-9
FURMAN SELZ INC.	SELZ	5.55	6	3-8
SHERWOOD SECURITIES CORP.	SHWD	6.28	6	3-8
SOUNDVIEW FINANCIAL GROUP	SNDV	5.64	6	4-8
SOUTHWEST SECURITIES INC.	SWST	3.46	4	2-7
TROSTER SINGER CORP	TSCO	5.55	5	3-7

MARKET MAKER	SYMBOL	AVG SCORE	MY EVAL	HI/LO FROM SURVEY
TUCKER ANTHONY INC.	TUCK	4.37	4	2-7
TEEVAN & CO., INC.	TVAN	5.00	6	2-8
UBS SECURITIES INC.	UBSS	4.91	6	3-6
VOLPE WEITY & CO.	VOLP	3.73	4	2-6
S.G. WARBURG & CO. INC.	WARB	4.28	5	3-6
WILLIAM BLAIR & CO.	WBLR	4.19	5	2-6
WHEAT, FIRST SECURITIES INC.	WEAT	4.19	5	2-7
WEDBUSH MORGAN SECURITIES	WEDB	4.55	5	3-7
WEEDEN & CO. LP	WEED	5.46	7	2-8
WERTHEIM, SCHRODER & CO., INC	WERT	5.19	6	3-7
WALLSTREET EQUITIES INC.	WSEI	4.00	4	2-6
WESSELS, ARNOLD & HENDERSON	WSLS	4.91	7	2-8

This chart represents only the opinion of the surveyed group. While all the respondents have years of SOES trading experience, in some instances there were wide discrepancies in the evaluation of a particular market maker. Use the chart only as an indication of other people's opinions. You soon will draw your own conclusions.

CHAPTER TWELVE

WHICH ARE THE SOES STOCKS?

Which stocks do SOES traders watch? In general, there is a primary list of stocks that meet the criteria of SOES trading. These stocks are actively traded with large public floats. They are followed by many brokerage firms and subject to many upgrades, downgrades, earnings forecasts, product analyses and other types of probing analysis. They usually trade a minimum of several hundred thousand shares daily, although Nasdaq volumes are usually grossly overstated. A SOES stock is highly visible and actively traded by many institutions, mutual funds, individuals and market makers. These stocks are often household names such as APPLE COMPUTER, MICROSOFT, INTEL, SNAPPLE (although recently delisted because of a merger), LOTUS, US HEALTHCARE, BOSTON CHICKEN, DELL COMPUTER, AMERICAN ON-LINE, NORDSTROM, NOVELL, ROADWAY EXPRESS, STAPLES, etc. Many other stocks are not household names, but are very heavily traded by the people who know about them. They are institutional favorites, have high volatility and great depth of market. Stocks such as Applied Materials (AMAT), Sybase (SYBS), (BNET), Biogen (BGEN), 3COM (COMS), Amgen (AMGN), Cordis Corp. (CORD), etc., are not household names but are extremely good stocks to trade and are followed by virtually every SOES trader in the business. The Nasdaq 100 list of stocks is a good starting point for the new SOES trader. Remember, monitor only as many stocks as you can efficiently or else you will see so many updates and changes as to make the data virtually meaningless.

Below you will find the list of the stocks found in the NASD 100 index. This index follows the 100 most prominent stocks traded in the Nasdaq market. With rare exception, they are all good SOES trading stocks.

NASDAQ-100 INDEX
AAPL - APPLE COMPUTER, INC.
ACAD - AUTODESK, INC.
ACCOB - ADOLPH COORS COMPANY
ADBE - ADOBE SYSTEMS INCORPORATED
ADCT - ADC TELECOMMUNICATIONS, INC.
ADPT - ADAPTEC, INC.
AESC - AES CORPORATION (THE)
AGREA - AMERICAN GREETINGS CORPORATION
AKLM - ACCLAIM ENTERTAINMENT
ALEX - ALEXANDER & BALDWIN, INC.
AMAT - APPLIED MATERIALS, INC.
AMGN - AMGEN, INC.
ANDW - ANDREW CORPORATION
APCC - AMERICAN POWER CONVERSION
ASAI - ATLANTIC SOUTHEAST AIRLINES
ASTA - AST RESEARCH, INC.
ATML - ATMEL CORPORATION
BGEN - BIOGEN, INC.
BMCS - BMC SOFTWARE, INC.

Nasdaq 100 cont'd
- BMET - BIOMET, INC.
- BNET - BAY NETWORKS, INC.
- BOBE - BOB EVANS FARMS, INC.
- BRNO - BRUNO'S INC.
- CALL - NEXTEL COMMUNICATIONS, INC.
- CBRL - CRACKER BARREL OLD COUNTRY
- CHIR - CHIRON CORPORATION
- CHRS - CHARMING SHOPPES, INC.
- CMCSK - COMCAST CORPORATION
- CNTO - CENTOCOR, INC.
- COMS - 3COM CORPORATION
- CPWR - COMPUWARE CORPORATION
- CRUS - CIRRUS LOGIC, INC.
- CSCO - CISCO SYSTEMS, INC.
- CTAS - CINTAS CORPORATION
- DELL - DELL COMPUTER CORPORATION
- DIGI - DSC COMMUNICATIONS CORPORATION
- ERTS - ELECTRONIC ARTS, INC.
- FDLNB - FOOD LION, INC.
- GENZ - GENZYME CORPORATION
- GIDL - GIDDINGS & LEWIS, INC.
- HBOC - HBO & COMPANY
- HCCC - HEALTHCARE COMPARE CORP.
- HONI - HON INDUSTRIES INC.
- IFMX - INFORMIX CORPORATION
- INEL - INTELLIGENT ELECTRONICS, INC.
- INTC - INTEL CORPORATION
- JBHT - HUNT TRANSPORT SERVICES, INC.

Nasdaq 100 cont'd
- KELYA - KELLY SERVICES, INC.
- KLAC - KLA INSTRUMENTS CORPORATION
- LDDS - LDDS COMMUNICATIONS, INC.
- LGNT - LEGENT CORPORATION
- LINB - LIN BROADCASTING CORPORATION
- LLTC - LINEAR TECHNOLOGY CORPORATION
- LOTS - LOTUS DEVELOPMENT CORPORATION
- LRCX - LAM RESEARCH CORPORATION
- MCCRK - MCCORMICK & COMPANY
- MCIC - MCI COMMUNICATIONS CORPORATION
- MLHR - HERMAN MILLER, INC.
- MMEDC - MULTIMEDIA, INC.
- MOLX - MOLEX INCORPORATED
- MSFT - MICROSOFT CORPORATION
- MTEL - MOBILE TELECOMMUNICATION
- NDSN - NORDSON CORPORATION
- NOBE - NORDSTROM, INC.
- NOVL - NOVELL, INC.
- ORCL - ORACLE SYSTEMS CORPORATION
- OSSI - OUTBACK STEAKHOUSE, INC.
- PAGE - PAGING NETWORK, INC.
- PAYX - PAYCHEX
- PCAR - PACCAR INC.
- PCCW - PRICE/COSTCO, INC.
- PHSYB - PACIFICARE HEALTHSYSTEMS, INC.
- PHYB - PIONEER HI-BRED INTERNATIONAL
- PMTC - PARAMETRIC TECHNOLOGY
- PRGO - PERRIGO COMPANY

Nasdaq 100 cont'd
- PTCM - PACIFIC TELECOM, INC.
- QCOM - QUALCOMM INCORPORATED
- QNTM - QUANTUM CORPORATION
- QVCN - QVC NETWORK, INC.
- ROAD - ROADWAY SERVICES, INC.
- RPOW - PRM INCORPORATED
- SIAL - SIGMA-ALDRICH CORPORATION
- SPLS - STAPLES, INC.
- SSSS - STEWART & STEVENSON SERVICES
- STJM - ST. JUDE MEDICAL, INC.
- STRM - STRATACOM, INCORPORATED
- STRY - STRYKER CORPORATION
- SUNW - SUN MICROSYSTEMS, INC.
- SYBS - SYBASE, INC.
- TCOMA - TELE-COMMUNICATIONS, INC.
- TLAB - TELLABS, INC.
- TYSNA - TYSON FOODS, INC.
- USHC - U.S. HEALTHCARE, INC.
- VCELA - VANGUARD CELLULAR SYSTEMS
- VKNG - VIKING OFFICE PRODUCTS INC.
- WMTT - WILLIAMETTE INDUSTRIES, INC.
- WTHG - WORTHINGTON INDUSTRIES, INC.
- XLNX - XILINX, INC.
- YELL - YELLOW CORPORATION

Perhaps of more interest is my other list of SOES trading stocks. This is the list followed by perhaps my most successful SOES trader ever. His success in SOES trading since 1989 has been the envy of virtually all of his peers and contemporaries. Out of respect for his privacy, I will not divulge his name but this is not important - his list is.

Remember new stocks come into play almost every day. I am a strong believer that SOES traders should ignore the business press and television reports and monitor them only to find new candidates for SOES trading. Check the most active lists and "stocks in play" (subject to takeover rumors or other meaningful events). This data is available on most quotation systems, as well as, newspapers and television. After a short period of time you will learn to customize your monitoring and develop your own style.

TRADER'S LIST

ABBY	BOCB	GENZ	LLTC	PCTL	SPLS
ACAD	BORL	GRND	LOTS	PELB	SSSS
ACTL	BROD	GYMB	LRCX	PITC	STJM
ADBE	CELS	HBOC	MCAWA	PMTC	STRL
ADPT	CHIR	HCCC	MCCS	PRGS	STRM
AGREA	CHPM	HDTC	MCIC	PRXM	STRY
AKLM	CMAG	HOME	MIDL	PSFT	SUNW
ALTR	COMS	HOSS	MLTF	PYXS	SVGI
AMAT	CORD	HTCH	MNCO	QCOM	SYBS
AMER	COST	ICST	MRDN	QHRI	SYMC
AMGN	COTTF	IDTI	MRNR	QVCN	THDO
ANDW	CRTV	IFMX	MSFT	REGA	TLAB
ASTA	CRUS	IMNR	MTEL	RHDS	TNCR
ATML	CRYS	IMNXD	NELC	RNBO	TOTE
BBBY	CSCC	INEL	NETG	ROAD	USBC
BEAM	CSCO	INTC	NGCO	SAFC	USHC
BELM	CSNO	KLAC	NOBE	SCIS	VCELA
BEST	DELL	KMAG	NOVL	SIAL	VLSI
BGEN	DIGI	KOIL	NVLS	SMED	WALL
BKSO	EGLS	KSWS	ORCL	SMLS	WAMU
BMCS	ERTS	LGNT	OSSI	SMSC	XLNX
BNET	EXBT	LIPO	OXHP	SPBC	ZENL

CHAPTER THIRTEEN

CONCLUSION

This guide might seem a bit simplistic for those used to heavy analytical, technical and fundamental analysis. Therefore, I leave the analysis to the "analysts". We SOES traders are just too basic a group for those heavy thinking analysts. We just grind out profits (or quickly absorb losses), enjoy our relatively short hours, enjoy the exhilaration and live the good life. If you are truly motivated to enter an exciting and rewarding new career or just want to liven up your monotonous day - SOES trading could very well be the answer. The only problem is that it is relatively so easy to learn you might think it could not possibly work. It does! Although I caution you that you should not devote financial resources to SOES trading that you cannot afford to lose. Get off your high horse, find out more and there is no question in my mind that you too will become a "bandit".